Orca Origins

# Powwow

Karen Pheasant-Neganigwane

## A Celebration through Song and Dance

ORCA BOOK PUBLISHERS

*Everything in the universe has a rhythm, everything dances.*

—Maya Angelou

**Library and Archives Canada Cataloguing in Publication**
Title: Powwow: a celebration through song and dance / Karen Pheasant-Neganigwane.
Names: Pheasant-Neganigwane, Karen, author.
Series: Orca origins.
Description: Series statement: Orca origins | Includes bibliographical references and index.
Identifiers: Canadiana (print) 20190169923 | Canadiana (ebook) 20190169931 | ISBN 9781459812345 (hardcover) | ISBN 9781459812352 (PDF) | ISBN 9781459812369 (EPUB)
Subjects: LCSH: Powwows—Juvenile literature. | LCSH: Powwow songs—History and criticism—Juvenile literature. | LCSH: Indian dance—North America—Juvenile literature.
Classification: LCC E98.P86 P44 2020 | DDC j394—dc23

Library of Congress Control Number: 2019947369
Simultaneously published in Canada and the United States in 2020

**Summary:** Part of the nonfiction Orca Origins series for middle readers. Illustrated with photographs, *Powwow* is a guide to the dance, music and culture of this Indigenous celebration.

*Orca Book Publishers is committed to reducing the consumption of nonrenewable resources in the making of our books. We make every effort to use materials that support a sustainable future.*

Orca Book Publishers gratefully acknowledges the support for its publishing programs provided by the following agencies: the Government of Canada, the Canada Council for the Arts and the Province of British Columbia through the BC Arts Council and the Book Publishing Tax Credit.

Edited by Merrie-Ellen Wilcox
Design by Dahlia Yuen
Front cover photos by Linda Roy, Ruth Bergen Braun and Shutterstock.com
Back cover photo by Linda Roy
Author photo courtesy of Karen Pheasant-Neganigwane

ORCA BOOK PUBLISHERS
orcabook.com

Printed and bound in China.

23  22  21  20  •  4  3  2  1

*To the Eighth Fire, and to those who work to build understanding
that will move us toward peace, harmony and healing.*

# CONTENTS

## Chapter Four:
## Powwows from Coast to Coast

Women's beaded top, designed and created by Northern Traditional dancer Kristol Abel (Anishinaabe; Ontario).

*Linda Roy*

My grandson Olin Osawamick (Anishinaabe/Nehiyaw) is a Grass dancer who's been dancing since he could walk.

*Brad Callihoo*

# *Introduction*

When I was a little girl, my family spent the summer holidays at my grandparents' home in northern Ontario. They lived on a farm in Wiikwemkoong, a First Nation on Manitoulin Island, far from the city where we lived. The farm was on a **reserve**, and my cousins, aunties and uncles lived there too.

Both of my parents had been sent to an **Indian residential school**, so they knew the hardships and trauma caused by it. They thought we would get a better education if we left the reserve so we could go to public school. We were the first generation to live away from our home reserve.

My cousins on the reserve had to chop wood for the woodstove to keep their home warm and haul pails of water in order to bathe. In our home in Toronto, Ontario, besides being able to flip a switch to get heat or turn a tap

My home on the Wiikwemkoong reserve sits in a field of wild strawberries. Strawberries are very important to me.

*Meryca Shawongonabe*

Fred Astaire and Ginger Rogers.
*RKO Radio Pictures*

My granddaughter Kallan
Pheasant-Neganigwane (Anishinaabe)
is a Traditional dancer.
*Robert Snache*

to get running water, we also had a television. Saturday morning cartoons made us laugh, but when the cowboy and Indian movies came on, I felt sad. The TV Indians did not look or talk anything like my relatives on the reserve. My grandma did not know how to speak English. My cousins spoke in **Anishinaabemowin** most of the time, not English. The Hollywood version of Indians also caused a lot of teasing and bullying by other kids in our city neighborhood. Life as the lone "Indian" family in the neighborhood was painful.

The good thing about television was that it gave me a window into dance. When I watched Hollywood dance musicals, I could leave my troubled reality and escape to another place. The most famous dancing couple at the time was Fred Astaire and Ginger Rogers. They would float across the floor, their graceful, fluid movement holding me in awe and taking me to a magical place. In the privacy of my bedroom I would imitate their dance and try to find that enchanted space for myself. Then I would swoop, swirl and twirl up and down our narrow hallway.

No matter how engaging their dips and swirls were, though, their dance was worlds apart from what I knew.

>>>

As soon as school was finished in June, we would start to get ready for the day-long drive north. The excitement of being home with my grandparents and other relatives would keep me awake the night before we left. There was also my grandma's soup and homemade pies to look forward to—and there was the powwow.

Hearing the drums and the power of the songs at the powwow, and being with so many other First Nations people, was incredibly exciting. I urged my mom and auntie to make me a "powwow dress" so I could dance too. It was as if once we put on our "Indian" dance clothes, a power took over us on the dance floor. The closer I moved to the dancing spirit, the lighter my feet would become. When I was little I would get lost among the dancers, hiding from the tourists who were watching. But as I began to feel the dance spirit, I would forget about the tourists. Those joyful dance moments were breathtaking. They were also an escape from the harsh realities of being Indigenous in the city where we lived. It wasn't dance as I had experienced it watching Fred and Ginger from afar on the television screen. It was a time of celebration and acceptance of identity, if only for a moment.

Even after everything they had been through at Indian residential school, my mom and dad had instilled in us pride in being Indigenous, in being **Anishinaabe**.

My grandparents Mary Jane Pangowish and Alfred Mishibinijima in 1976. My Mishomis (grandfather) is holding my daughter, Sophie. Her dad, Junior Pheasant, is behind them.

*Courtesy of Karen Pheasant-Neganigwane*

My granddaughter Francesca Pheasant (Anishinaabe) is a Fancy Shawl dancer. She's wearing beadwork that I designed and created for her.

*Robert Snache*

Children in the Shawl
Dance in the late 1970s.

*Ron Spence*

It wasn't easy living off the reserve, though, with our brown skin. I felt sad when I was teased and bullied for being "Indian." We just did what we were supposed to do—work or go to school—and kept silent. But when we went home to the reserve for the summer, I would get to dance, play and just be myself, without keeping silent. Powwow time was the time to celebrate our identity. Being around powwow dance always made me feel beautiful.

Later, when I was a teenager, powwow dance began to mean something different for me. Through the **American Indian Movement**, with its songs, headbands and political marches, dance became an expression of political power. Reading Dee Brown's book *Bury My Heart at Wounded Knee*, about the history of Indians in the American West, made me feel both sorrow and an immense pride in the fact that Indian people were still around—that we still had our songs, our dances and some of our ceremonies.

It was also around this time, in the early 1970s, that my parents took me to my first large powwow away from Manitoulin Island. It was at Mount McKay, south of Thunder Bay, Ontario. The powwow grounds there were outdoors, with campsites all around the dance area. The camp and dance areas both had a kind of magnetism— full of laughter, visiting and big pots of simmering stew. As I grew older and became a seasoned dancer, I came to realize the value and importance of the camp life, too, and how it kept our culture strong.

In 1982 my sister and I went with our young children to the largest powwow in Canada, the World Assembly of First Nations, north of Regina, Saskatchewan. It was my first powwow outside of the Great Lakes region. I was awed, not only by the hundreds of dancers, the power of

the songs, the breathtaking dance arena and the huge campsite with majestic family tipis that encircled it, but also by the spirit that was present everywhere. At the end of the first day of the powwow, amid the evening songs and conversations, I knew I had found my true place as a dancer.

During my years as a young single parent, I learned that staying true to Indigenous cultural traditions involves relationships. Federal government policies required children to be removed from their parents and communities for 10 months of the year, sometimes even for the whole year, to attend Indian residential schools, which traumatized individuals, caused families to break down and damaged Indigenous **kinship systems** (the web of relationships that connects people and defines their

The Saturday afternoon grand entry, Kainai Indian Days, Stand Off, Alberta. That's me on the left, in my jingle dress.
*Ruth Bergen Braun*

Children are introduced to the dance arena at a very young age. Tamia is the daughter of Alexis and Nugget Bull Bear (Siksika, Blackfoot).
*Ruth Bergen Braun*

Waiting for the grand entry, among the food vendors, Kainai Indian Days.

*Ruth Bergen Braun*

Head dancers Ardel Scalplock (Siksika/Blackfoot; Alberta) and me at a National Museum of the American Indian powwow, Washington, DC, 2005.

*AB Historic/Alamy Stock Photo*

responsibilities to one another). Powwow culture and its practices became a way to restore relationships and to balance contemporary life and cultural traditions. Realizing this changed my life. This was what I wanted for my children and me—kinship and cultural nourishment through dance.

I spent the next 30 years traveling with my children to powwows across North America and, occasionally, abroad. Sometimes we had only a jar of peanut butter, some bread and a sleeping bag in our pickup truck. Sometimes a performance would include a stay in a hotel with meals and a bit of pay. Whether we were dancing at a powwow, the 1994 Discovery of the Americas celebration in Mexico City, a dance conference in Australia or the 1996 Summer Olympics in Atlanta, Georgia, dance provided much more than an income. It gave my children a secure footing in their lives as Indigenous people, something that wasn't available to them living in a city during those years.

My parents didn't powwow-dance. My grandparents didn't powwow-dance. It wasn't until I was an adult that I fully understood the reason for dance and the power of songs. I wanted to make sure my children understood the stories behind the dances and the songs. I took them traveling across North America to see, hear and feel the blessings of powwow culture, not only of Anishinaabe people but also of the Blackfoot, Cree, Haudenosaunee (Iroquois), Dakota, Nakoda, Lakota, Miccosukee, Mandan, Arikara and Hidatsa, Meskwaki, Pueblo and Navajo, to name just a few.

The songs and dances are an important part of my life story. But the story I am going to tell in this book is about how Indigenous Peoples' ceremonial songs and dances had to be hidden and then how they became a different kind of dance—a dance of celebration that evolved into what we now call powwow dance.

My son, Grass dancer Jesse Osawamick.
*Perry Mah*

## A Note about Terms

In Canada, the European settlers and colonial governments used the word *Indian*, and it continues to be used by the federal government in some legal contexts because of the **Indian Act**. However, many Canadians are now using the term *First Nations* instead of *Indian*, and *Indigenous Peoples* for First Nations, **Métis** and Inuit. In the United States, however, the terms *Native American* and *American Indian* are used.

Because this book is about the powwow in both Canada and the United States, I have used the terms *Indigenous Peoples* and *tribal nations* when I am talking about groups in both countries, *First Nations* for groups specifically in Canada, and *Native Americans* for groups in the United States. (There are other terms that are different in the two countries, like *reserve* in Canada and **reservation** in the United States.) I have used *Indigenous people* when I am referring to individuals rather than groups.

But it's important to remember that these are very broad, general terms. And, like people from Europe who preferred to be known as Italian, Greek, Polish and so on rather than just *European*, Indigenous Peoples prefer to be known by the name of their nation. For example, I am Anishinaabe, which means "First Peoples" or "Good People." I recommend that you find out the names of the tribal nations in your region and learn how to pronounce them.

In 1976 I was a Fancy Shawl dancer.
Notice the old-style wraparound leggings.

*Courtesy of Karen Pheasant-Negonigwane*

# ONE

# Origins of POWWOW CULTURE

> Every Indian or other person who engages in, or assists in celebrating or encourages, either directly or indirectly, another to celebrate, any Indian festival, dance or other ceremony of which the giving away or paying or giving back of money, goods, or articles of any sort forms a part, or is a feature, whether such gift of money, goods or articles takes place before, at, or after the celebration of the same, and every Indian or other person who engages or assists in any celebration or dance of which the wounding or mutilation of the dead or living body of any human being or animal forms a part or is a feature, is guilty of an indictable offense.

—INDIAN ACT, amended 1895

My grandson Torin Pheasant-Neganigwane, Grass dancer, Kainai Indian Days.

*Ruth Bergen Braun*

**The first powwow that took place** on my home reserve, Wiikwemkoong, was in 1960. Powwow culture was quite new to Indigenous communities back then, because until 1951 it had been illegal for Indigenous Peoples in Canada to practice their culture and ceremonies, which included dance. As well, because my parents had attended Indian residential school, where they were always shamed for their Indigenous identity, there wasn't much Indigenous culture or tradition in my home. As a young child, before I went to the powwows, my only understanding of what *Indian* meant was from those Hollywood "cowboy-and-Indian" shows on TV.

*Children in residential schools were severely punished for speaking their own language or expressing any other part of their culture.*

## Colonization

Every culture has ways of marking important events like births and deaths, marriages and changes of season. Indigenous Peoples celebrated these occasions with specific songs and dances—at least, they did until these cultural practices were made illegal. In both Canada and the United States, European settlers gained political control over Indigenous Peoples and their lands by creating new ways of living and governing. This is called *colonization*.

An important part of colonization was *assimilation*, which meant making Indigenous people stop being themselves and become just like the settlers. Most were forced to speak the settlers' language rather than their own and convert to the European religion, Christianity. Once occupying the entire North American continent, Indigenous Peoples now had to live in much smaller areas, called reserves in Canada and reservations in the

An Indian residential school.
*Shingwauk Residential Schools Centre, Algoma University*

Indigenous children at the Old Sun Indian residential school in Gleichen, AB, on the Blackfoot reserve, in the 1940s.

*General Synod Archives, Anglican Church of Canada*

United States. And in Canada, all Indigenous children were forced to go to schools called Indian residential schools (or in some cases Indian day schools) to be "educated" in settler ways—and assimilated. In the United States, many Indian children had to attend boarding schools run by governments for the same purpose.

## The Indian Act and the Pass System

In Canada, the Indian Act came into force in 1876. Its purpose was assimilation. Among other things, it defined who was an Indian, where Indians could live and what they could and couldn't do. It banned essential

A traditional Potlatch was both a ceremony that included songs and dances and a way to share wealth among all members of a community.

Louis Riel (seated, center) and members of his provisional government, 1870.

*Archives of Manitoba*

ceremonies like the **Potlatch** and the **Sun Dance**. The Indian Act has changed over the years, but it is still in place today.

Around the same time as the Indian Act was being written, the Canadian government was worried about political unrest, both on the Canadian Prairies and on the Great Plains to the south.

When a vast area of land once controlled by the Hudson's Bay Company was transferred to the Canadian government in 1869, Métis leader Louis Riel led an uprising, known as the **Red River Resistance**, and attempted to form a new government. This led to the creation of the province of Manitoba, but it also meant that the Canadian government saw Riel and his many followers as outlaws. Riel continued to resist the government and was finally charged with treason and hanged in 1885.

Meanwhile, Sitting Bull and Crazy Horse, leaders of the Sioux peoples of the American plains, strongly resisted the US government's efforts to confine their people to reservations. The resistance led to the **Battle of the Little Bighorn** in 1876, in which the United States Army's 7th Cavalry Regiment was defeated and General George Custer was killed. Sitting Bull and some of his followers escaped to Canada in 1877, where they started small communities in southern Alberta, Saskatchewan and Manitoba. (Although many of them returned to the United States when the buffalo disappeared in Canada, a few Sioux communities still remain today.)

Sitting Bull, who led his Hunkpapa Lakota people through years of resistance to US government policies.
*Library of Congress*

A pass from 1932, allowing a man to leave his reserve for two weeks of trapping.
*Provincial Archives of Saskatchewan*

Faced with all this unrest, the Canadian government created the **pass system** in 1885 as another way to control First Nations people in western Canada. The system forced people to stay within their reserves. If someone wanted

Powwows are generally a place of kinship and family—both immediate and extended family.
Mark James

to visit relatives or attend ceremonies at another reserve, they would have to request a pass from the **Indian agent**, a representative of the Canadian government whose job it was to oversee reserves. The pass system, which was not part of the Indian Act or any other law, remained in place for more than 60 years.

## The Wild West Shows

For tribal nations throughout North America, song and dance gatherings were an essential part of culture, with many important purposes—spiritual, ceremonial, social, political and educational. So as part of their efforts to control and assimilate Indigenous Peoples, governments in both Canada and the United States tried hard to stop people from singing and dancing. Many Indigenous people continued to perform their songs and dances in secret, at the risk of being put in jail. But something else happened at the same time.

New spiritual traditions, like the Ghost Dance of many Plains tribal nations, gave people hope when it seemed their culture was facing extinction.

*The Ghost Dance by the Oglala Lakota at Pine Ridge Agency, drawn by Frederic Remington from sketches taken on the spot. Library of Congress*

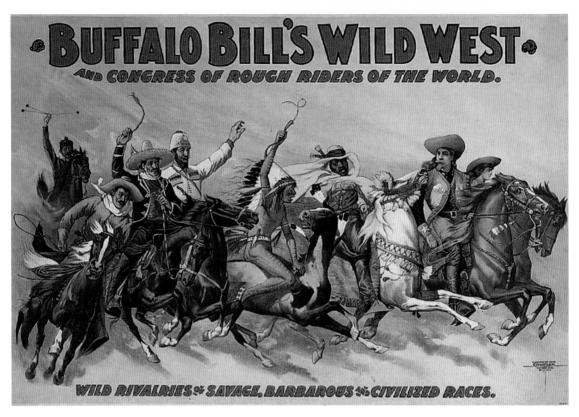

The Wild West shows became the only opportunity for men to leave reservations and earn money for their poverty-stricken families.

*Library of Congress*
*LC-USZ62-53794DLC*

Since non-Indigenous people expected that the Indian would now simply "vanish," some people thought it would be good to celebrate these vanishing cultures through cowboy-and-Indian shows. The shows, which were a combination of theater production, battle reenactments, and song and dance, drew huge non-Indigenous audiences.

Perhaps the most famous of these circus-like productions was Buffalo Bill's **Wild West show**. Operated by Buffalo Bill Cody, who was from Nebraska, the show traveled throughout North America and Europe between 1883 and 1913. It was a huge hit wherever it went. There were two command performances for Queen Victoria in England, as well as shows for other royalty throughout Europe. Cody also took his Wild West show to the Trans-Mississippi International Exposition in Omaha, Nebraska, in 1898 and to the World's Columbian Exposition in Chicago, Illinois, in 1893. The show was wildly popular—so much so that in Omaha it had to be moved to a different location to hold all the spectators.

Even though the Indian songs and dances had been banned, businessmen like Buffalo Bill Cody were using them to make money. Since the shows were theatrical, the Indians who performed had to add color to their costumes and increase the tempo of their songs and dances. Indigenous leaders didn't intend to turn their songs and dances into theatrical spectacles for the public, but the reservations had no other economy to sustain their families. Their songs and dances became the only way to earn an income for their families.

Contemporary powwows have their own speciality dance categories. Here, young Shawl dancers choreograph a "Team Dance" routine that they will compete with.

*Linda Roy*

*The Anishinaabe people of the Great Lakes region made baskets from the wood of black ash trees. Both of my grandmothers were champion split-ash basket makers. My mother told me that there was always excitement in the air before the fall fair on Manitoulin Island, with everyone wondering who would win the basket title that year. One of my grandmothers could bring great color patterns into her baskets, while my other grandmother was able to weave intricate designs into hers.*

A split-ash basket made by my Nokomis (grandmother), Mary Jane Pangowish (Odawa). She was well known for her work, which was collected by museums like the Royal Ontario Museum.

*Crystal Migwans*

To the public, these shows looked like Indians singing and dancing. But to the singers and dancers it was much more: it was one of the only opportunities they had to gather off their reserves and reservations, to discuss ways of dealing with government controls. Performing in the shows had other benefits too. At a time when Indigenous people were not allowed to leave their reserves to earn money, and there were no jobs on reserves and reservations, being a performer was the only way they could get permission to leave *and* earn some money. And it provided a chance for them to get together and quietly share their cultural practices and knowledge among themselves.

In the end, the Wild West shows helped preserve the songs and dances of Indigenous cultures and also changed them into something new.

## Fall Fairs

In Canada, First Nations people also performed their songs and dances in exhibitions and fairs for local people and tourists. Once again, the Canadian government used laws to try to suppress these activities. In 1914 this was added to the Indian Act:

Any Indian in the province of Manitoba, Saskatchewan, Alberta, British Columbia or the Territories who participates in any Indian dance outside the bounds of his own reserve, or who participates in any show, exhibition, performance, stampede or pageant in aboriginal costume without the consent of the Superintendent General of Indian Affairs or his

A Wolastoqiyik boy harvesting potatoes on a farm in New Brunswick.

*Topley Studio/Library and Archives Canada/PA-010754*

authorized Agent, and any person who induces or employs any Indian to take part in such dance, show, exhibition, performance, stampede or pageant, or induces any Indian to leave his reserve or employs any Indian for such a purpose, whether the dance, show, exhibition, stampede or pageant has taken place or not, shall on summary conviction be liable to a penalty not exceeding 25 dollars, or to imprisonment for one month, or to both penalty and imprisonment.

But in agricultural areas, like my home territory in the Great Lakes region, First Nations people in the early 1900s often recieved farming equipment from the government and adopted a farming lifestyle. And an important part of that lifestyle was the fall fair, which included exhibitions of the best livestock, like cattle, sheep and chickens, and the best produce and crafts. At these fairs First Nations people were encouraged to dress in leather, beads and feathers, representing the "vanishing Indian," rather than in their standard farm clothes like any other farmer.

My granddaughter Kallan was a Shawl dancer when she was younger.

*Manuel Sousa*

## A Growing Powwow Culture

In the United States, where the government had been trying hard to stop Native Americans from dancing since the 1880s, many tribes by the early 1900s were beginning to fight the government for control of their dances. And with many Native American men joining the army to fight for the United States in both the First and Second World Wars, the government realized it couldn't stop Native Americans from doing Sun Dances to pray for their men.

During and after the Second World War, more and more dances were held in Native American communities, especially in the west. More people had cars by then, and public transportation was making it easier for people to travel from community to community. By the 1950s and '60s there was a growing powwow culture.

## Banned No Longer

In 1951 the Canadian government made some changes to the Indian Act. Among other things, it was no longer illegal for First Nations people to practice their customs and ceremonies, have gatherings or appear off-reserve without permission of the Indian agent.

By then the Indian Act and other government policies had had a large impact on First Nations. Because of the Indian residential schools, Indigenous children were ashamed to participate in ceremonies, and **Elders** were afraid to share and promote their traditional knowledge. Some of the old ceremonies and rituals were no longer used or had been altered.

### Powwow Fact

Anishinaabe **knowledge keeper** Edward Benton-Banai wrote an important book called *The Mishomis Book: The Voice of the Ojibway*. In it he described a prophesy known as the Seventh Fire, which describes how the people had to hide their traditional knowledge because of colonization, and how younger generations will need to reclaim that knowledge: "In the time of the Seventh Fire a Osh-ki-bi-ma-di-zeeg (New People) will emerge. They will retrace their steps to find what was left by the trail. Their steps will take them to the elders who they will ask to guide them on their journey. But many of the elders will have fallen asleep. They will awaken to this new time with nothing to offer. Some of the elders will be silent out of fear. Some of the elders will be silent because no one will ask anything of them. The New People will have to be careful in how they approach the elders. The task of the New People will not be easy."

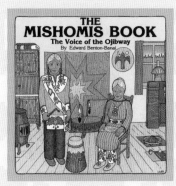

THE MISHOMIS BOOK
The Voice of the Ojibway
By Edward Benton-Banai

Southern Buckskin dancer Red Plume Woman (Sharon Roberts, Chickasaw Nation).

*Dan Gooden*

*Many urban schools today have powwow clubs that meet during lunch hours or after school. They usually host an end-of-year powwow. Community members often come to the schools to teach powwow dance and donate or make dancewear. Clubs like this are especially important for urban Indigenous students who are trying to recover their Indigenous identity and heritage.*

In part due to poverty, though, and also as a means to get out to visit their relatives, First Nations people continued to dance at local fairs and exhibitions, sometimes asking non-Indigenous people to host them at those events. In western Canada, First Nations soon began to host their own summer events called "Indian Days." In Anishinaabemowin, they were (and in some places still are) referred to as *Wii Gitchi niimi'idiwin* (Big Dances).

Soon after the Indian Act was changed, teachers and other people from my home community of Wiikwemkoong began to attend Indian Days in the Prairie provinces. They wanted to learn how to share their traditional cultural practices, which had been hidden for so long, with their neighboring communities.

During the 1960s powwows became increasingly popular events during the summer months on reserves. American reservations just south of the Canadian border, which were making money from the oil under their land, hosted large celebrations. Reservations like Fort Peck in Montana hosted two or three major powwows every year. This drew First Nations people from Canada across the border to participate and compete in these events and encouraged them to host their own powwows.

## Twelve Months a Year

Powwows have continued to grow since then—and they've grown a lot! Until about 20 years ago they took place only in the summer. They were a kind of homecoming event, mostly on reserves, hosted by the community or by families, where people who lived off-reserve would come back to visit and celebrate with their relatives. Colleges and universities sometimes hosted powwows in the spring too.

Now there are powwows 12 months a year. Powwows take place in many of the major cities across Canada and the United States, both within the city limits and nearby. And in addition to Indigenous communities, agencies, friendship centers, schools, colleges and universities hosting local powwows, corporations such as casinos, particularly Indigenous casinos, sponsor and host powwows year-round. In the 1980s there would usually be between 100 and 200 dancers at a powwow. Today it is common to see 800 or more dancers at a big competition powwow!

Children from across North America share each other's tribal knowledge, creating long-lasting friendships, engaging in healthy competition, and teaching and learning their unique dance styles.

*Linda Roy*

## Powwow Fact

**Bannock and Fry Bread**

Bannock and fry bread are often made using the same recipe, but one is baked and one is fried. I was recently invited to a friend's house for soup and bannock. My friend's niece was the bannock maker, and I watched as she meticulously measured the ingredients.

This stirred a childhood memory of my grandmother. The picture that came to mind was of her outstretched hand. She would use a coffee cup to scoop flour out of the bag, pouring it into her cupped hand before putting it in the bowl. After doing this a few times, she poured a bit of baking powder onto her palm, followed by a tiny sprinkle of salt. Next, she stirred the dry ingredients in the bowl and formed a small well in the middle, into which she poured either canned milk or water. She mixed everything together to get the texture she wanted. Finally she kneaded the dough on the table, making it the right size and shape for either baking or frying. All this was done in silence, with a sustained, intent focus.

My favorite part, though, was eating the hot bannock or fry bread with fresh honey or Grandma's jam on it. That's what I remember best!

This Jingle dress features strawberries in its design. For some eastern tribal nations, strawberries have both healing and ceremonial uses.

*Courtesy of Karen Pheasant-Neganigwane*

# My Father's Story

**My father was born in 1926** and was his mother's youngest baby. When he was about five or six years old, before he was taken away to Indian residential school, he went with his mother to the back of a field, far away from any prying Indian agents. He remembered seeing the big drum set up in the middle of the grassy field, and a few well-respected men from the community who sang and hosted the proceedings.

My father said his mother "wore a shawl around her shoulders, but not a shawl like you see now at powwows... There were no flashy colors, just a simple little shawl over her shoulders. She would stand on one spot, dancing up and down..." His eyes glistened as his voice trailed off in reflection.

When my dad told me this, I was dancing full-time and teaching dance in different communities across Canada. He recognized the changes that had taken place between his childhood and the contemporary powwow. He didn't quite understand the rise in popularity of the public powwow shows. He only knew the spiritual practice of the drum and dance, something that he was raised to keep silent about in order to keep them alive when they were banned. But he recognized that other ways were needed to keep cultural practices alive, even if in a less solemn way.

My father, Wassegijig (Moses Lavallee; Anishinaabe), experienced a lot of trauma but understood the value of balancing Indigenous values and contemporary urban practices.

*Courtesy of Karen Pheasant-Neganigwane*

My son Jesse and his wife, Jingle Dress dancer Kyla Sanderson (Nehiyaw), with their son Olin at the Rama Powwow, Rama, ON.

*Robert Snache*

# TWO

# WHAT IS POWWOW CULTURE?

*I danced past my wounds, beyond the trauma of our collective intergenerational pain and forward to the hopes of a good future for my people. It was an empowering spiritual victory. Now, whenever I dance I know how important it is to bring my spirit along. And, how powerful it can be when people bring that energy together at the same time. This is the power of powwow.*

—*NAHNDA GARLOW,*
Onondaga Beaver Clan, Six Nations
of the Grand River

My niece Lisa Marie Lavallee (Anishinaabe) in her jingle dress.

*Robert Snache*

**Powwow culture has changed a lot** in the last few decades, and there are now many different kinds of powwows, from smaller, traditional, local ones held on

My granddaughter, Shawl dancer Francesca Pheasant, wearing beadwork that I created for her with my favorite strawberry design.

*Linda Roy*

reserves and reservations to large competition powwows that take place in stadiums and casinos.

Traditional powwows don't cost anything to attend. Competition powwows sometimes charge an admission fee. Some powwows focus just on the songs and dances, but others include other activities, like rodeos, fashion shows, music awards, midway rides and dance "specials"— exhibitions of dances from specific regions or peoples.

But no matter how small or large the powwow, it is still the same in spirit. It's still a celebration through song and dance, and it's public and open to anyone, even people who have no experience. People go to powwows to have a good time—to hear the songs and dance or watch the dancers, see friends, share meals, tell stories and remember the past. There are certain things that are part of every powwow. We're going to look at some of them in this chapter.

Western powwows in places like Crow Agency, Montana, and many Alberta communities often include other events, such as rodeos.

*Bert Crowfoot*

During intertribal songs and dances, all audience members are welcome to participate. Dance outfits are not required. It's a time to feel the songs and join the other dancers as they dance in their own styles.

*Linda Roy*

## The Powwow Grounds

*The powwow grounds are blessed, usually by Elders, before the event begins. Prayers, songs and the burning of sage or tobacco make sure that the space is empowering.*

Whether the event takes place in a field, an arena or a casino, the powwow grounds are laid out in a similar way. Usually there is a series of concentric circles or layers, with the area for the dancers at the center, sometimes called the **dance arbor**, and the drums either right in the middle or beside the dance area. Around that is space for Elders and the dancers' family and friends and, outside that, space for other spectators. Often there will be a campsite encircling the area, where people pitch their tents or tipis or park their campers.

And there are always vendors. You'll find food vendors selling traditional foods based on their grandma and grandpa's favorite recipes, as well as the standard fair food—burgers and fries. Other vendors sell arts and crafts, including T-shirts, beadwork, craft supplies such as beads and leather, and supplies for making dance **regalia** (the clothing, footwear and other special items that dancers wear). Sometimes dancewear and regalia are also available to purchase.

Not that long ago, many families came to powwows prepared to stay in a tipi encampment.
*Evo Danchev/Getty Images*

## The Emcee

Emcees Allan J. Manitowabi
(Anishinaabe; Wiikwemkoong)
and Vince Byle (Anishinaabe;
Bemidji, Minnesota).

*Robert Snache*

Every powwow has a master of ceremonies, or an **"emcee."** In the past the emcee was like a town crier for the powwow camp, telling all the news of the event. It was a role that had to be earned before it would be assigned.

Today emcees often hold an important position in their community. Many are knowledge keepers in their communities, following the traditional cultural practices of their people, as well as having a Western education.

At a powwow the emcee speaks through a microphone, announcing what is happening and what will happen next, introducing the dignitaries and the dancers, encouraging people to join in the dancing and sometimes sharing stories of the community and Indigenous history.

> Veterans are given special roles at powwows, like carrying flags and offering prayers. This is a way to honor them and show respect for their courage and service.

The grand entry, Kainai Indian Days.
*Ruth Bergen Braun*

## The Grand Entry

All powwows today start with an opening parade, or what we call the grand entry. The grand entry was adopted from the Wild West shows of the late 1800s, which usually began with a similar parade of all the performers. But it also reflects the processions to treaty signings and other important events in the 1800s, when warriors and chiefs proudly displayed their regalia and their military strength.

No matter where you attend a powwow in North America today, if it's a two-day powwow, there will be a grand entry at 1 and 7 PM on Saturday, and again at 1 PM

Indian taco, a favorite at many North American powwows.

*Ruth Bergen Braun*

on Sunday. If it's a three-day powwow, there also will be a 7 PM grand entry on Friday.

Today the chiefs, local politicians or other dignitaries, and military veterans (people who have been in the armed forces) might lead the grand entry, followed by the flag bearers and then all the dancers, sometimes in a particular order of men and women, boys and girls, or senior and younger dancers. Generally, a respected **Drum** is selected to sing the grand-entry songs.

When all the dancers have entered, everyone stands for the ***flag song***, which is usually that of the nation hosting the event. (Each tribal nation has a flag song, which is like a national anthem.) Then there are the ***victory songs***, followed by an opening prayer and welcome from the host community, sometimes in their own language.

## Powwow Fact

### Powwow Food

Feasts have always been a source of pride and unity, connecting families, generations, tribes and nations, so it's not surprising that food is an important part of every powwow.

A popular powwow food is the Indian taco, with layers of seasoned ground beef, grated cheese, lettuce and sour cream stacked on fry bread, a flat bread that is fried or deep-fried in oil or lard. At the same time, though, fry bread is a painful reminder of forced removal and oppression, as well as a source of illness today. Indigenous people started making fry bread about 150 years ago, using food rations provided by governments, including white flour, processed sugar and lard. Today fry bread is thought to be one of the many causes of the high rates of diabetes among Indigenous Peoples in North America.

As tribal nations look for ways to improve the health of their communities, the menus at powwows now include Indigenous foods that are truly traditional, like hominy corn, wild rice and wild meats.

## Powwow Fact

### Victory Songs

Many of the songs you'll hear at a powwow retain a deep spiritual and philosophical meaning and importance. In the summer of 2016, I joined the other older women dancers in the grand entry at the annual Prairie Island Wacipi (pronounced wa-chee-pee—another word for powwow in the Dakota language) in Welch, Minnesota. Generally, victory songs have a standard drumbeat and composition. This time, though, the songs stirred a strong reaction in me, and I didn't know why. They seemed to affect the others too—hundreds of dancers from all over the continent—because the dance took on a new form. It was a dance of unity and firmness, but with a gentle grace to the low steps.

Later I was sitting with friends in the campground, and we heard some Sioux people talking about those songs. It turns out they were the *Waktegli Waci*, the original victory songs sung after the Battle of the Little Bighorn in 1876, when Sitting Bull defeated General Custer and the United States Army's 7th Cavalry Regiment.

And finally the dancing begins, usually with an ***intertribal dance*** where everyone is welcome to join in.

## Competition

If the powwow is competitive, the dance categories are broken into age, dance-style and gender groups. (We'll look at the different kinds of dances in chapter 3.) The competition is run by one or more head judges, and the other judges might be dancers from a different category. The judges use a point system, giving the dancers scores for their expression and style, footwork and regalia. They might also ask them to dance a second time with a different kind of footwork.

Chippewa Grass dancer Adam Nordwall (Shoshone/Chippewa). He dances a unique style and wears floral beaded designs.
*Linda Roy*

Matayaz Mark (Stoney Nakoda Sioux; Morley, AB) has been dancing since he could walk.

*Ruth Bergen Braun*

> *Indigenous Peoples in general have a different value system, which is based not on how much money they make or the number of things they own, but rather on how much they share or give away. Giving away prized possessions shows a person's kindness, thoughtfulness and sincerity. People who receive gifts are not expected to give anything in return but are simply to remember the gift giver in their prayers.*

Women dancers leading younger dancers in the evening grand entry, Rama Powwow.

*Robert Snache*

Dance competitions are a bit like the Olympics—you can't just show up and expect to compete, even if you are the best gymnast or skater in your community. You have to compete and succeed at different levels before you become an established powwow dancer. At each level there are many considerations besides the color, splendor and choreography of the dance.

In addition, there are Drum contests, which are competitions for singers based on song knowledge, skill and creativity.

## The Giveaway

A *giveaway* ceremony often takes place on the last day of a powwow. At a powwow, gifts may be given to show the hosts' appreciation to visitors who have traveled a long way to take part in their event. A giveaway may also be held in memory of someone who has died or to welcome new powwow dancers, usually children.

The ceremony begins with a dance by those who will be giving gifts—usually members of the powwow organizing committee or the host tribal nation, although anyone can take part. After the dance is finished the emcee calls the names of those who have been chosen to receive a gift. Smaller gifts may be distributed among the rest of the people present.

Gifts can include everything from blankets, quilts, leather goods, horses and money to groceries and kitchenware. Giveaways are planned for weeks and months before the powwow, and the gifts are made or purchased, sometimes at great expense to the families.

## Stories

Although powwows are celebrations through song and dance, they are also a place where important stories are told, stories you won't find in a book or an encyclopedia or by googling.

Stories containing thoughtful cultural knowledge may be shared in different places at a powwow—at the camps encircling the powwow grounds, in the circle around the dance arbor where families sit with relatives to visit, laugh and share stories of the past, and in the dance arbor. Sometimes a respected knowledge keeper or Elder may be invited to share their life experiences and Indigenous knowledge.

Taco in a Bag—same toppings as for the Indian taco, but with a bag of corn chips instead of fry bread.

*Brent Hofacker/Shutterstock.com*

> When making this recipe as well as the other recipes in this book, be sure an adult is around to supervise.

# Taco in a Bag

*Taco in a Bag is a little healthier and easier to make than an Indian taco, because it doesn't include the fry bread. Have an adult cook the hamburger and chop the vegetables or supervise you closely if you already know how to do this. Makes 4 servings.*

### Ingredients:

1 pound hamburger, cooked with taco seasoning

4 small bags corn chips (2.5 or 3 ounces each)

Lettuce, chopped or shredded

Tomato, chopped

1 cup shredded or grated cheddar cheese

Salsa

Sour cream

### Directions:

1. While the hamburger is being cooked, gently scrunch up the corn chips, leaving the bags unopened.
2. Using scissors, cut the corners off the bags and slit them open along the side edge.
3. Spoon an equal amount of cooked hamburger, lettuce, tomato, cheese, salsa and sour cream into each bag.
4. Eat with a fork!

## Restoring Kinship

The impacts of colonization stretch far beyond the loss of our languages and cultures. In Canada, Indian residential school and what is known as the **Sixties Scoop** also destroyed Indigenous family and kinship systems. (During the Sixties Scoop, rather than being sent to residential schools, Indigenous children were taken from their families and communities to be adopted or fostered by non-Indigenous families.) With generation after generation of children not being raised by their parents, grandparents, aunts and uncles, and often being abused

Parents preparing Tiny Tot dancers for their big moment.

*Bert Crowfoot*

My son Jesse prepares Olin for his dance contest.
*Brad Callihoo*

by Indian residential school staff and even by adoptive or foster parents, children didn't learn how to be parents, grandparents, aunts and uncles in the traditional way.

The last Indian residential school didn't close until 1996, and the practices of the Sixties Scoop continued into the 1980s. First Nations families and communities are still recovering as we continue to reclaim our roles, responsibilities and social practices.

The time I spent traveling with my children on the powwow trail taught me that the songs and dances and stories shared at powwows are not just about identity and culture. Powwows also help to restore our families and kinship systems.

Bear Creek Anishinaabe Drum, from Sault Ste. Marie, ON (Nathan Isaac, John Syrette, Wayne Silas Jr., Mike Tegosh, Kevin Syrette, Gabe Gaudet and Nitanis Kit Largo), at Central Michigan University, Mt. Pleasant, MI.
*Eric Brouwer*

# THREE

# Powwow Songs and Dances

> We have a beautiful life...we have songs for
> when we are celebrating, when we are happy,
> when we are sad, we have songs for mourning,
> for births...we have songs for everything.
>
> —*ELI SNOW,* (Stoney Nakoda),
> traditional dancer, grandson of Chief John Snow

Eli Snow (Stoney Nakoda). Men's Northern Traditional red dance accessories are created from porcupine quillwork.

*Bert Crowfoot*

**Songs have always been important** to our people. Long before the arrival of powwow culture, there were songs for many of the events in our lives—births, initiation ceremonies, welcoming ceremonies, marriages and burials. Today we still have many of these songs, and we have powwow songs and dances as well. In this chapter, I'm going to tell you about some of our main powwow songs and dances.

Some songs use "vocables," syllables that aren't words referring to specific things. Vocables help people share their songs among people who speak different Indigenous languages.

Young hand drum singer and Grass dancer Pahquis Trudeau (Anishinaabe) on the Wiikwemkoong shoreline.
*Linda Roy*

## Drums

When tribal nations began to reclaim their cultural practices (in Canada, this was after the Indian Act was changed in 1951), it was hard to find an original-style drum. Government policies had required that ceremonial and other cultural items be taken away and sometimes burned—in the hope and expectation that they would never be used again.

People resorted to creating drums from old marching-band bass drums, sometimes with the original plastic skins on them or with skins from animals like cow or elk, to give the beat a deeper sound. Others made their drums entirely by hand. Today most drums are decorated with traditional designs, and they might be wrapped in embroidered cloth or deerskin.

In our languages, the drum is referred to almost as a person. Most tribal nations have societies that uphold the drum and song **protocols** and obligations, which includes ensuring that ceremonies and feasts are done at certain times of the year. Specific members of these societies are responsible for the drum protocols, whether organizing the sacred feasts, dressing the drum or creating and composing songs.

Following a drum protocol is a bit like sitting at someone else's dining room table. You wouldn't just walk into a person's house and sit at their table or help yourself to the food—even if you knew them. Either you would wait to be invited or you would hint that you wanted to eat at their table. It's the same with a drum. A person cannot invite themselves to take a drumstick and start singing at a drum. There are layers of restrictions, or protocols, to follow first.

## The Drum

A Drum is a group of men—three to twelve or sometimes more—and, in some regions, women. Generally, it is the men who sing at the drum. If there are women, they stand behind and sing. At powwows the regular members of the Drum can be joined by friends and family members, as well as members of other Drums.

Drums practice regularly between powwows. They learn to keep a steady beat and sing with precision at a volume that matches the singing. Good singers also know all the songs by heart. A good Drum combines all these things to create harmony, which in our culture means a balance between the singers, the drum and the song.

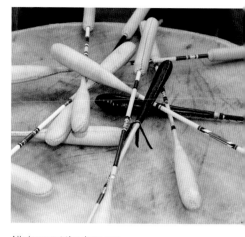

All singers at the drum use these drumsticks.
*Len Collection/Alamy Stock Photo*

Drums are usually handmade by a local drum maker, using natural animal hides, sometimes with local tribal designs.
*Bill Perry/Shutterstock.com*

Men's Buckskin dancers of the Blackfoot Confederacy in Alberta. Generally, Men's Buckskin dancers are the elder dancers of a nation.

*Ruth Bergen Braun*

## Dance Categories and Styles

The beauty of powwow dance is that there is a place and recognition for everyone and every age group. When I first started dancing and traveling in the 1970s, there were only two dance styles, Traditional and Fancy, and generally only two or three age categories—child, teen and adult. Today there are usually eight to twelve dance categories and four to six age categories.

The youngest category is Tiny Tots—toddler to age five. At both traditional (noncompetitive) and competition powwows, the Tiny Tots generally dance all together (boys and girls) shortly after the grand entry and receive a small monetary gift, usually around five dollars each. Next comes the boys and girls category, for ages six to twelve, then the teens, ages thirteen to seventeen, and finally the adults, ages eighteen and up. In recent years some larger powwows have also begun to divide adults into junior and senior (Golden Age) adults.

The Traditional and Fancy dances can have different regional styles. New dance styles, like the women's Jingle Dress Dance and the men's Grass Dance, were introduced to the powwow dance floor in the 1980s. Let's take a look at some of these styles and their origin stories as I have learned them over my years as a dancer.

## Men's Traditional Dance

Evolved from older forms of war dances, the men's Traditional Dance may tell a story about war or a hunting expedition, or it might imitate animals, such as horses, birds or buffalo.

Campers and RVs are replacing tipis and tents (Kainai Indian Days).

*Ruth Bergen Braun*

Clayton Old Elk (Apsáalooke;
Crow Agency, MT).
*Bygone Collection/Alamy Stock Photo*

The dancer wears a beaded vest, a war shield and a **roach** made from stiff porcupine hairs on the head. A single, circular **bustle** (a spray of eagle or manmade feathers) is worn on the back. Most dancers carry some sort of staff or dancing stick. The colors and designs used in each dancer's regalia can symbolize their clan or family or represent their Indigenous name.

The dancers tell a story through their steps, as warriors bending low to the ground and peering cautiously about or as hunters moving in for a kill in a successful hunt. They rarely dance backward as they perform, as this would be seen as a retreat, and in the original manner or style there would be no turning in a full circle.

A newer form of men's Traditional Dance is the Contemporary Dance, where outfits are brighter and flashier and the dancers move more wildly, which includes going backward or turning in full circles.

Many male dancers wear a roach made of porcupine hair. Each type of men's dance has a unique and intricate style.
*Jamey Penney-Ritter/Shutterstock.com*

Patrick Mitsuing (Cree; Saskatchewan).
*Sandra Crowfoot*

## Men's Fancy Dance

The men's Fancy Dance originated in the southern United States, and it was intended as entertainment. The dancers' fast movements and the bright colors of their regalia create an exciting spectacle.

Men's Fancy dancers wear two bustles on their backs. They also wear a cape made of cloth and ribbon that may be fully beaded and matching front and back aprons. In addition, they wear a roach, fur leggings and bells.

The men's Fancy Dance is an endurance test. With its complex steps and body movements, all done in time with a very fast drumbeat, the dance requires participants to be physically fit and well coordinated. Dancers can make

up their own steps, often bringing their knees up to their chest or dropping to the ground and leaping back up to their feet, all without missing a beat.

## Men's Grass Dance

The men's Grass Dance is a favorite of mine, as I have two sons and two grandsons who are Grass dancers. The Grass Dance was originally a sacred ritual, part of a long, complex ceremony performed by warrior societies among various tribal nations of the Plains. There are several different versions of the origin of this dance, coming from various places in Canada and the United States. Some nations believe it was a healing dance, especially for a sick child. Others say it was used to bless the ground, flattening the grass before a feast or ceremony took place. In either case, it was a *ceremonial dance*.

My son Matthew Pheasant has been a Grass dancer since he was a child.

*Manuel Sousa*

Dancers long ago wore outfits made with only natural materials, such as grass, porcupine quills and hair. Grass dancers today still use some of these things, but now they have added beadwork, bells and brightly colored fringes made with ribbons or yarn to their outfits. Each wears a belt, cuffs, headband and roach with two eagle feathers or a set of feather plumes. The outfit is designed to move with the dancer, enhancing his motions as he moves his hips, arms, head and shoulders in harmony with his dance steps. Grass dancers imitate the gentle swaying of grass on a windy day and must show balance, endurance, coordination and gracefulness.

The Grass Dance is divided into two categories at powwows—Old Style and Freestyle. Old Style has a reflective, serene and calming dance expression while

Freestyle (also known as "Contemporary") is a quicker, more agitated and creative form of movement.

## Women's Traditional Dance

The women's Traditional Dance is a dignified, graceful and modest dance intended to reflect a dancer's strength, pride and respect for her family, relatives and friends.

A unique style of women's Traditional Dance is the stationary dance, which originated among the Dakota/Nakota people in their small gatherings of long ago. The women would stand and bounce gently to the drum in honor of the family or relatives for whom the song was sung. They wore their most elaborate quilled, beaded and decorated dresses and accessories, created from traditional family designs or ones seen in dreams. The dresses reflected the hard work and patience required to make such a complicated thing.

Most women dancers today carry a fan, usually made of eagle feathers, sometimes raising it gracefully to show respect and honor as they dance.

Bringing in the New Year at the Wiikwemkoong New Year's Eve powwow, with my youngest granddaughters, Lilly and Mattlyn. Both are dancers.

*Courtesy of Karen Pheasant-Neganigwane*

### Powwow Fact

**Prairie Chicken Dance**

The Prairie Chicken Dance, or Pihewisimowin, danced only by men, is said to have originated on the Prairies and is practiced by many First Nations there. Traditionally the dance was part of a healing ceremony held in a **longhouse** and begun with a pipe ceremony. The dancers would form a circle around two fires and begin to move slowly around the circle, mimicking the prairie chicken's springtime mating dance. Men who had never taken part in the dance before were required to give gifts, and the Elders who received the gifts in turn gave prayers for the dancers.

Today the Prairie Chicken Dance is becoming popular at powwows across the continent.

Prairie Chicken dancers, Kainai Indian Days.

*Ruth Bergen Braun*

The Haudenosaunee Smoke Dances come from southern Ontario and New York State.

*Mark James*

Amber Old Horn (Apsáalooke; Crow Agency, MT), Crow dancer. Apsáalooke Crow style has its own distinct dancewear and dance movement, and generally only Apsáalooke have the right to do this dance.

*Bert Crowfoot*

Some powwows have separate categories for cloth and buckskin dresses. And a recent addition to the women's Traditional style is the Scrub or Appliqué style. It is a dance of the Menominee, Ho-Chunk and Anishinabek women from the central and western Great Lakes region. The women's dresses include intricate ribbon work and appliqué patterns, and the dance steps are different from those of other Traditional styles.

## Women's Fancy Shawl Dance

The women's Fancy Shawl Dance originated in the south-central United States and has a couple of different interpretations. Some dancers see it as symbolizing the life of a butterfly. A butterfly emerges from her cocoon and blooms into a beautiful, fragile creature. She then lives freely and quietly, flying around her habitat, displaying beauty and grace. The story I'm more familiar with is that the late Gladys Jefferson (Crow Agency, United States) created

Alva Snow (Stoney Nakoda),
Shawl dancer and daughter
of Eli Snow.

*Denis Thorp*

Fancy Shawl Dance in the late 1950s as a way for women to be more expressive on the dance floor.

Women's Fancy Shawl dancers' outfits are beautifully intricate. They include a beaded cape with matching leggings, moccasins and hairpieces. Dresses are usually calf length, and the dancers wear a shawl across their shoulders.

The Fancy Shawl dancer moves her body in perfect time with a fast drumbeat, showing grace, endurance, agility and lightness in her steps, with her shawl swaying and swirling in perfect harmony with her body.

## Women's Jingle Dress Dance

I first saw the Jingle Dress Dance at a powwow in Thunder Bay, Ontario, in the mid-1970s. At that time, it was generally danced by the older women at the ceremony lodge, known as the Round House. I later learned that this was the dance of the *Ogitchidah Kwe* (Warrior Women) society of the Anishinaabe people of the Lake of the Woods

Asiniw Iskwew (Irene Oakes, Nekaneet First Nation).

*Bert Crowfoot*

Jingle Dress dance special at Kainai Indian Days. (That's me in the green dress.)

*Ruth Bergen Braun*

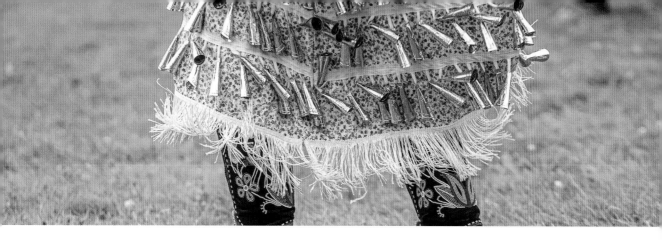

area in Ontario and Minnesota. Today all ages can do the Jingle Dress Dance, even Tiny Tots, and it is revered at both competition and traditional powwows across North America.

As with other dances, there are various stories about the origins of the Jingle Dress Dance. The common theme is that the jingle dress originated in a dream and was intended to bring healing. Today the jingle dress is adorned with several rows or layers of tin ornaments that vibrate when the dancer moves. When many Jingle Dress dancers move in unison to the drum songs, the ornaments create an almost mystical sound. The ornaments are usually made from lids of soup cans or snuff tins, rolled into a cone.

Originally the Jingle Dress Dance involved a graceful lifting of the feet off the dance floor, with steps a bit like the Charleston dance from the 1920s. But today there are two separate styles—what I would call Original and Contemporary. The Original style has a modest, light choreographic style, and the dress includes an underskirt to reflect the dancer's modesty. The Contemporary style is a bit like the Fancy Shawl Dance, with spins, twirls and complicated footwork, performed with or without eagle fans and feathers. The dress doesn't include an underskirt.

Originally, the cones on a jingle dress were made from the lids of snuff cans. These days, dancers order them from craft suppliers.
*Robert Snache*

Iconic Jingle Dress Dance Nokomis, Evelyn Thom (Anishinaabe; Whitefish Bay, ON). Now in her 80s, she danced until recently.
*Bert Crowfoot*

Dancers enjoy chatting and watching friends and family members dancing during intertribal dances. My daughter, Sophie (left), and Deanne Hupfield are both dance educators.

*Robert Snache*

## Intertribal and Social Dances

All powwows include dances where everyone can join in and have fun. Intertribal dances include a variety of different songs, both slow and up-tempo. Depending on the tribal nations' protocol, the dance circle moves either clockwise or counter-clockwise. For example, the Haudenosaunee and some tribal nations in British Columbia and Washington State generally move counter-clockwise. It's always best to watch the dancers and listen to the emcee so you know which direction to dance in!

**Social dances** take different forms, like the Round Dance, Rabbit Dance, Old Moccasin Dance and Canoe or Fishing Dance. One of the most popular is the Haudenosaunee Smoke Dance. It was originally a war dance in which only men participated, but women later created their own unique version of it.

Ceremonial dances, like the Maple Syrup, Strawberry, Bean, Sun, and Moon Dances, are kept for the longhouse, where ceremonial activities take place. They are generally not done in public places.

*Every song has an introduction, and then the beat changes and the dancing starts. Many powwow songs and dances have been adapted from those of different tribal nations. Men are said to dance with a certain amount of pride and even arrogance, while women dance in a more graceful style. But every dancer has a different style.*

# ᎾStrawberry Drink

*Strawberries are important as food and medicine for many Indigenous Peoples and are often available during summer powwows. Makes 4 servings.*

## Ingredients:

1 pint strawberries

4 cups cold water

Sweetener (maple syrup, honey or sugar) to taste

## Directions:

1. Wash the strawberries, put them in a large bowl, and mash them with a potato masher or a fork.
2. Add the water and mix.
3. Taste. If you think it should be a little sweeter, add a tablespoon of sweetener and taste again. Add and taste until it's sweet enough for you.
4. Use a ladle to spoon the drink into glasses.

# My Drum Story

Birdie Eagle Speaker's sister, Evelyn. Their Drum, Blood Travelers, sang original-style Blackfoot songs.

*Harry Palmer*

In the mid-1980s I was living near the Blood, or Kainai, reserve in southern Alberta. As an Anishinaabe woman, I learned that Drums in that region were often family based and included women drummers. These were mature women—mothers—who sang with their families. As an Anishinaabe woman from Ontario, I had mostly seen men singing and sitting at a drum.

One day the lead singer, Birdie Eagle Speaker, walked up to me and handed me a drumstick. This was an honor not to be taken lightly. I was a visitor in another tribal region, and I had been accepted with open arms by many of the Blackfoot people. Should I be upholding the protocols from my own nation? In the end, I could not refuse the invitation.

My time with the Drum was short, but it was filled with good company, laughter and singing. At Drum practices I learned the origins, history and styles of many songs. Besides warrior songs, there were Chicken Dance songs, Sun Dance songs, Chief songs—the list was endless. At a powwow, when another Drum started up a song, someone at our Drum would tell the story or the origins of that song, including who made the song, whether it was a song passed on to someone else and perhaps how a gift or exchange was required to gain the right to sing the song.

When I went back to my home powwow in Wiikwemkoong, I wondered if maybe there had been a change and women were singing with Drums there too. I told my Eagle Speaker Drum story to one of the local knowledge keepers. I had hoped that my experience in Alberta might lead him to invite me to sing at his Drum, since I'd known him for a long time. As I shared the details of my western Drum and singing experience, he listened with his head down, sometimes nodding in acknowledgment. When I finished my story, he walked away. I understood that walking away was his humble way of saying no to a place for me at the Drum.

Meanwhile, a large number of young women in shorts and other summer attire had been gathering around the drum area. The master of ceremonies for the powwow was Eddie Benton-Banai, an important knowledge keeper (see sidebar on page 21). His voice now came sharply through the sound system, asking the young women to leave the drum area. He told the story of how the Drum was given to the men by a spirit woman in a sacred way, and that the Drum was to be used for specific purposes and taken care of in a precise way. I believe these kinds of stories come to people for a reason and at an important moment. I realized that no invitation would come anytime soon for me to sing with my Drum brothers.

That was over 30 years ago. In my home region of the Great Lakes, there are still no women at the big drum. In some places there are exceptions based on local protocols. And women in some urban areas have adopted the use of the hand drum. I've asked drum keepers about this, and many are not sure how or when this occurred.

Traditionally, drums are kept in a special place— a drum house. When they are taken out for singing, they are treated as living beings and given gifts of tobacco.

Sonny Eaglespeaker (Blackfoot) hand drum singing at the Lethbridge International Peace Pow-wow.
*Ruth Bergen Braun*

Serene Goodwill,
granddaughter of Irene Oakes,
at the Manito Ahbee Pow Wow.

*Robert Dearden*

# FOUR

# POWWOWS FROM COAST TO COAST

When I teach people who are going to become teachers, I start by asking where each student is from. They usually say they are Canadians. When we dig deeper, they might say their country of origin is, for example, France, Italy, Greece, Poland, Ukraine, India or China. I point out to them that no one identifies themselves simply as "European" or "Asian"—they identify a specific country.

Similarly, when you ask an Indigenous person about their identity, they generally say that they are Anishinaabe, like me, or from another tribal nation. And there are so many! For example, here in Alberta there are 46 First Nations, as well as Métis people. In British Columbia, there are 198 distinct First Nations and more than 30 Indigenous languages. The same is true for other provinces in Canada, as well as in much of the United States.

The joy of powwow friendships.
*Linda Roy*

There are hundreds of tribal nations in North America. All have their own unique traditions and history. But they also have some things in common, and today most, though not all, have powwow culture in their communities.

My family has danced in powwows from one end of the continent to the other, from Nova Scotia to British Columbia in Canada and from Florida to California and Washington in the United States. In this chapter we'll look at powwows in different regions of North America.

## Central Canada

As a child, I danced only in my home community of Wiikwemkoong, on Manitoulin Island. The powwow there has been held since 1960, always on the first weekend

*Back in the 1960s and '70s, there were only a few powwows. Today powwows are held 12 months a year. Powwow traveling is extensive and expensive. Families often pool together as singers, dancers and powwow technicians. Some dancers dance full-time and become known as the "circuit" powwow people. There are dancers who dance in all kinds of powwows, competitions, shows and other performances, and performance dancers who dance only in shows and exhibitions. And like full-time dancers everywhere, they spend a lot of time training, creating dancewear and working on their choreography.*

Young Haudenosaunee Smoke dancers. The Haudenosaunee Smoke Dances have a style of singing and dancing that is very different from other powwow dance styles.

*Mark James*

of August, which is a holiday. It's the oldest powwow gathering in eastern Canada.

As I got older and began to travel more, I learned that other tribal nations had their own distinct cultural practices. In Ontario, I watched Haudenosaunee longhouse songs and dances. Their drum was smaller and was held by a solo singer—very different from the large powwow drum and songs I had grown up with. The dancers also dressed differently, and the songs had a different beat. Today the Haudenosaunee Smoke Dances are seen mostly at powwows in Ontario and New York State.

The most popular and longstanding powwow in southern Ontario is at Six Nations of the Grand River (in the community of Ohsweken) on the last weekend of July. Another large powwow takes place near Montreal, Quebec, at Kahnawake, in early July. Both powwows have a huge number of vendors, selling not just arts and crafts but also traditional foods such as corn soup, wild rice and Indian tacos.

## Powwow Fact

### Feeding Visitors

Feeding visitors has always been an important practice for Indigenous communities. In the late 1980s I went to a powwow at Whitefish Bay, which is in the Lake of the Woods region in northwestern Ontario. A major part of the event was a feast held by the Naotkamegwanning First Nation on the Saturday afternoon. Whitefish is an important food in the region, and the host Drum and their family members barbecued enough whitefish to feed the entire gathering—all the dancers and singers and their families!

The Elbow River Camp at the Calgary Stampede.
*Jeff Whyte/Shutterstock.com*

## The Canadian Prairies

The Peguis First Nation, a little north of Winnipeg, Manitoba, has an annual event known as Treaty Days. The powwow is just one part of the week-long festivities, which also include fastball and slo-pitch tournaments, a golf tournament, concerts and art exhibits, a triathlon, canoe races, a talent show, a parade and fireworks. A highlight for me is the jigging contest. Jigging is a Métis dance that came to the community long before the powwow.

Other powwows that have been happening for a long time in Manitoba are at Long Plain First Nation, Sandy Bay First Nation and Sioux Valley First Nation. The annual Manito Ahbee Festival in Winnipeg includes an Indigenous music conference.

In Saskatchewan, powwows and other cultural celebrations happen year-round. The First Nations University Powwow at the University of Regina is Canada's longest-running competition powwow. It is considered the opening powwow of the season, taking place at the end of winter term in April.

Alberta's oldest and largest powwow event began in 1912 as the Calgary Stampede and Indian Village. The Stampede takes place in the home community of Treaty 7 First Nations—the Tsuut'ina and Blackfoot Confederacy nations. Today the Indian Village, now known as the Elbow River Camp, features 26 tipis representing the five Treaty 7 nations: Kainai, Tsuut'ina, Stoney Nakoda, Siksika and Piikani. In addition to the powwow competition, there are traditional games and storytelling venues and a traditional foods booth.

*The eagle feather is of great spiritual importance to Indigenous Peoples. In some territories, if an eagle feather falls on the ground at a powwow, only a wounded veteran can pick it up.*

Don McKay (Dakota; Sioux Valley, MB), Northern Traditional dancer.
*Ruth Bergen Braun*

Women's Traditional dancers Edna and Rachel Bad Eagle (Niitsitapi) wear Blackfoot-style hats reflecting the Treaty 7 agreement.

*Ruth Bergen Braun*

*Wild rice is actually a kind of grass that grows in water. Indigenous Peoples have been harvesting wild rice in North America for around 12,000 years.*

Each of the Treaty 7 Nations, and many other First Nations in Alberta, hosts its own powwows. The Women's Traditional dance has a unique character in Alberta: Siksikaitsitapi (Blackfoot) women (from the Kainai, Siksika and Piikani Nations) sometimes dance wearing large felt cowboy hats. I once heard a powwow emcee explain that the Treaty agreement that was signed said the leaders' wives would receive a hat. The Treaty specified that "at the signing, each chief and councillor would receive a suit of clothing and a Winchester rifle, while chiefs also would get a medal and flag. Thereafter chiefs and councillors would get a suit of clothing every three years." (A suit included a new hat!) In Canada, Siksikaitsitapi women are the only Traditional dancers who wear the felt hat—in recognition of the Treaty 7 agreement.

# The American Northern Plains

A special part of powwows in the Northern Plains of the United States is the Crow Parade Dance, also called the *Ashéeleetaalissua*, or Dance Through Camp. It is based on a ceremony that was a spiritual gift to the Apsáalooke people of the Northern Plains.

According to tradition, a warrior went to fast in the mountains. After several days he saw his people stop doing their activities and become various birds. Their leaders were young eagles, and they flew in a circle around the camp. The people were happy, and their hearts sang. When the warrior returned to camp, he told his people what he had seen. Since that time, whenever the Apsáalooke break camp, they perform the Dance Through Camp. This dance is a blessing and a prayer for future good camps where people are happy and successful.

Women's Northern Traditional dancers have different styles according to their nation. The two dancers on the right are Crow dancers, and the two on the left are Northern Plains-style dancers, but all are Cloth dancers.

*Rainer Grosskopf/Getty Images*

## Powwow Fact

### The Three Sisters: Corn, Beans and Squash

Many tribal nations, especially in eastern North America, traditionally grew corn, beans and squash. These vegetables are often called the Three Sisters, because when grown together, they grow better. Corn needs lots of nitrogen, which is produced by beans, and squash plants spread and prevent weeds from growing. When eaten together, they are very nutritious, providing a perfect balance of starch (carbohydrates), protein, fiber and important nutrients like vitamin A. At powwows, depending on the region and season, you will often find food vendors offering delicious and healthy Three Sisters soups and stews.

The Three Sisters: corn, beans and squash.
*igorsmas8/Shutterstock.com*

Roberta J. Kirk (Tenino/Wasco/Dine) with a patlapa, a ceremonial hat of the Pacific Northwest.

*Natalie Kirk*

The grand entry at the Kamloopa Powwow in Kamloops, BC.

*Emily Riddell/Alamy Stock Photo*

## The Pacific Northwest

The largest and oldest powwow in British Columbia is the Kamloopa Powwow. Hosted by the Tk'emlúps te Secwepemc people, it began in 1979 and is held every August in Kamloops. The powwow takes many of its elements from its Treaty 7 neighbors in Alberta. But at Kamloopa and other powwows in British Columbia, Washington and Oregon, you will likely see dancers in the traditional wear of the Pacific Northwest, which includes button blankets and cedar hats. The designs on these blankets and hats represent a person's clan, achievements or status within their community.

Other important powwows in the Pacific Northwest are the Julyamsh Powwow in Coeur d'Alene, Idaho, and the Spokane Tribe Labor Day Pow Wow, in Spokane, Washington. Since salmon is very important to Pacific Northwest coastal nations, salmon is served at most powwow feasts in the region.

Denny Medicine Bird
(Cheyenne/Arapaho; Oklahoma).

*Victoria Johnson/Skye Breese Photography*

## The Southwest

A special part of powwows in California today is Bird Singing. The singers, all men, line up on one side, accompanying their songs with handmade gourd rattles, and the dancers face them. As the men sing and create the rhythm with their rattles, the dancers facing them reply in kind of call-and-response style.

There are 67 tribes in Oklahoma, each with its own cultural heritage. These tribes bring a southern flair and interpretation to their dance styles, which feature a quick tempo and bass singing.

Gourd dancers in Gallup, NM.
*Donovan Shortey/CC BY-SA 3.0*

At powwows in Oklahoma and other southwestern states, you might see Gourd Dances before, after or between intertribal dances. Unlike the intertribal dances, where everyone can join in, dancers have to earn the right to be in the Gourd Dance.

Traditionally, many tribes held Gourd Dances, including the Ponca, Comanche, Cheyenne and Kiowa, who revived the dance. Today the gourd may be a real gourd, a stainless-steel salt shaker or even a tin can, decorated with leather, beads, string, feathers and horsehair. The dancers wear a ribbon shirt, buckskin leggings or pants, a sash around the waist, a Gourd Blanket made of red and blue wool over their shoulders, and either boots or moccasins. They move around the circle, slowly dancing and shaking their gourds. When the song shifts to a louder, stronger beat, the dancers stop and lift their heels as they shake the gourds strongly.

## The East

At powwows in Florida, home to the Seminole and Miccosukee Tribes, you might be lucky enough to see a Stomp Dance. Like some of the other dances described in this chapter, the Stomp Dance isn't a powwow dance but might be performed during supper breaks.

There is no drum in the Stomp Dance. The men sing as they dance, and the women provide the beat with shakers attached to their legs. Those who participate in the Stomp Dance wear their best Indian patchwork clothing. The fabric is made of brightly colored strips and geometrical shapes sewn together and is used for jackets, shirts and capes.

The Stomp Dance is part of the Green Corn Ceremony, a four-day gathering held each year by many tribes in

Seminole–style skirts, from the Seminole tribes of Florida.
*Juanmonino/Getty Images*

Florida and the Carolinas and all the way up to Maine to mark the season of renewal and thank the Creator for providing food and life.

## The Midwest

In the mid-1980s I danced away from my home region quite often, and one area that I spent a lot of time in was the American Midwest. The territorial battles caused by colonialism resulted in Anishinaabe, Menominee, Meskwaki, Dakota and Ho-Chunk people settling in Minnesota and Wisconsin. The presence of Anishinaabe people there provided some familiarity, and the Midwest became a tranquil place for me to camp and dance, even though there were other, less-familiar local tribal practices to learn.

Like other tribal nations, the Ho-Chunk people (formerly referred to as the Winnebago) have their own unique style of song and dance expression. Their dances, which we call a Woodland style, are a recent addition to the powwow dance floor. The dancewear is generally filled with floral woodland designs and patterns, often on black velvet, which was a prized possession in the nineteenth century.

## Attending a Powwow

As we saw in chapter 1, powwows arose out of North American tribal nations resisting colonial policies, laws and institutions, starting in the late 1800s, and refusing to abandon their cultural traditions. Today the powwow is a place where both Indigenous and non-Indigenous people can come together in peace and harmony to celebrate tradition—and, for some, a place where they can be introduced to Indigenous cultural knowledge.

If you have never attended a powwow and you would like to, there are several ways to do it. First, you could attend a powwow for a day as part of a school field trip or as a tourist. You could watch the grand entry, see some of the dancing, check out the vendors and eat some powwow food, such as corn soup, Indian tacos or blanket dogs (wieners wrapped in dough), and then return home. Another option is to take in the whole experience over two or three days, and either camp or stay in a hotel.

Whichever way you choose to attend a powwow, it's important to be respectful and follow **powwow etiquette**. Although some customs may vary from region to region, group to group and even year to year, the basic rules remain the same.

Dorothy "Pocahontas" Thunderchild (Cree) with raffle tickets at an Alberta powwow.
*Bert Crowfoot*

Indian residential schools broke family relationships, but today powwow culture brings together people of all ages, providing intergenerational family time for Indigenous communities.
*Linda Roy*

Theda NewBreast (second from right) and her mother, Betty N. Cooper (far left), of the Niitsitapi Women's Head Dress/Kaamipoisaamiiksi Society, with my daughter, Sophie, and me at the Kainai Christmas powwow.

*Courtesy of Karen Pheasant-Neganigwane*

# A Final Word from the Author

I said in the introduction that when I was a child attending the powwow on my home reserve of Wiikwemkoong, just watching the powwow dance made me feel beautiful. When the men sang around the drum, I could feel the power and energy move throughout my body. It felt like a blessing. Today I am grateful; the drum songs still make me feel beautiful. To me as a child, summertime was dance time. To me as a grandma, summertime is still dance time. Dance time is being with family, my grandchildren and friends.

As an educator working with urban Indigenous students, I have come to understand that many Indigenous people still do not have the connection with family and community that is their birthright whether because of Indian residential schools or the Sixties Scoop in Canada, or other colonization policies in both Canada and the United States. The child welfare system of Canada continues to take Indigenous children away from their families, community and cultural practices. For many of those who have had their identities taken away or, through no fault of their own, have not been able to know their culture, powwow culture serves as a stepping-stone to the reclaiming of their Indigenous identity.

***Mino-bimaadiziwin!***

Grass dancer Bodie Nordwall (Shoshone/Chippewa), Rama Powwow.

*Robert Snache*

# GLOSSARY

**American Indian Movement**—a group founded in 1968 in the United States to address issues like treaties and racism; between 1969 and 1971, the group led several important protests and occupations

**Anishinaabe**—a group of tribal nations in Canada and the United States with similar languages and culture, including the Potawatomi, Algonquin, Odawa, Saulteaux and Ojibwe peoples

**Anishinaabemowin**—the language of the Anishinaabe people

**assimilation**—an important part of colonization that involved forcing Indigenous people to speak the settlers' language and convert to their religion

**Battle of the Little Bighorn**—the 1876 resistance of the Sioux peoples, led by Sitting Bull and Crazy Horse, to the United States government's efforts to confine them to reservations; the United States Army's 7th Cavalry Regiment was defeated and General George Custer was killed

**bustle**—a circle of eagle feathers that men wear on their backs in the Traditional Dance

**ceremonial dance**—a dance that is generally not done in public places like powwows but in longhouses, where ceremonial activities take place

**colonization**—migration into new territory by a group of people who then take control of the people there and their lands by creating new ways of living and governing, as the European settlers did to Indigenous Peoples in North America

**dance arbor**—the dance area at a powwow

**Drum**—a group of three to twelve, or sometimes more, men—and in some regions women—who sing around a drum at powwows

**Elders**—people who are respected for various reasons, such as their age, wisdom or cultural knowledge

**emcee**—the master of ceremonies at a powwow

**flag song**—a kind of national anthem for each tribal nation

**giveaway**—an event that often takes place on the last day of a powwow, with gifts given to show appreciation to visitors, in memory of someone who has died or to welcome new powwow dancers, usually children

**Indian Act**—a law that came into force in Canada in 1876, defining who was an Indian, where Indians could live and what they could and couldn't do

**Indian agent**—an agent of the Canadian government whose job it was to oversee Indian reserves

**Indian residential school**—school that Indigenous children were forced to attend in order to be "educated" in settler ways and assimilated; in the United States, many Indian children had to attend boarding schools run by governments for the same purpose

**intertribal dance**—part of a powwow where everyone is welcome to dance

**kinship system**—the web of relationships that connects people and defines their responsibilities to each other

**knowledge keepers**—Indigenous people who have knowledge of, wisdom from and experience with the traditional cultural practices of their people

**longhouse**—a building or structure where ceremonies are held; considered a sacred area

**Métis**—Indigenous people in Canada whose ancestors were French, Scottish and First Nations

**Mino-bimaadiziwin**—an Anishinaabemowin term wishing someone a "good life"—not in a material sense but in a holistic way, bringing together body, mind, spirit, family and community

**pass system**—a way to control First Nations people, created by the Canadian government in 1885, by forcing them to stay within their reserves

**Potlatch**—a ceremonial feast of great importance to tribal nations of the Pacific Northwest, banned by the Canadian government between 1884 and 1951

**powwow etiquette**—the basic rules to follow and respect at a powwow

**protocol**—a set of rules, restrictions and procedures to make sure certain practices are followed in the correct way

**Red River Resistance**—an 1869 uprising in what is now Manitoba, sparked by the transfer of a vast area of land from the Hudson's Bay Company to the Canadian government

**regalia**—in powwow culture, all the clothing, footwear and other special items that dancers wear

**reservations**—small areas of land on which American Indians were forced to live by the government in the nineteenth century

**reserves**—small areas of land on which First Nations were forced to live by the Canadian government in the nineteenth century

**roach**—a headpiece made from stiff porcupine hairs, worn by men in the Traditional Dance

**Sixties Scoop**—the Canadian government's practice in the 1960s of taking Indigenous children from their families and communities to be adopted or fostered by non-Indigenous families, rather than sending them to Indian residential schools

**social dances**—dances at a powwow, like the Round Dance and the Rabbit Dance, that everyone is welcome to take part in

**Sun Dance**—an important cultural ceremony among the tribal nations of the Plains, honoring the sun and individual bravery

**victory songs**—songs sung at the beginning of a powwow and that often have deep spiritual and philosophical importance, sometimes because they were first sung after a major battle

**Wild West show**—a show produced by Buffalo Bill Cody that traveled throughout North America and Europe between 1883 and 1913, featuring songs and dances of the "vanishing Indian"

Grass dancer Adam Nordwall (Chippewa) and his daughter, Traditional dancer Nicole Nordwall (Shoshone/Chippewa).

*Brad Callihoo*

# RESOURCES

## Chapter One

*Print*:

Gray Smith, Monique. *Speaking Our Truth: A Journey of Reconciliation*. Victoria, BC: Orca Book Publishers, 2017.

Joseph, Bob. *21 Things You May Not Know about the Indian Act: Helping Canadians Make Reconciliation with Indigenous Peoples a Reality*. Port Coquitlam, BC: Indigenous Relations Press, 2018.

*Online*:

BearPaw Media Productions. "Understanding Aboriginal Identity." Video, 20:48. 2015. youtube.com/watch?v=IcSnbXmJ9V0

Lucitana, Donna. "Buffalo Bill" (Episode 4 of *The Real Wild West*). Video, 46:32. Greystone Communications/Arts and Entertainment Network, 1992. pbs.org.wgbh/americanexperience/films/cody

Oklahoma Historical Society, Film and Video Archives. "American Indian Dances at Indian City USA." Video, 10:09. 1950s. youtube.com/watch?v=LRSBmdzQ99I

School District 27 (Cariboo-Chilcotin, British Columbia). "Canadian History and the Indian Residential School System." Video, 22:15. 2014. youtube.com/watch?v=6-28Z93hCOI

Williams, Alex. *The Pass System*. Tamarack Productions, 2015. thepasssystem.ca

## Chapter Two

*Online*:

Elliott, Alicia. "Celebration, Resilience and Food: What to Eat at a Powwow." theglobeandmail.com/life/food-and-wine/celebration-resilience-and-food-what-to-eat-at-apowwow/article35287067

Garlow, Nahnda. "A Guide to Powwow Season in Canada." *WestJet Magazine*, June 2018. westjetmagazine.com/story/article/a-guide-to-powwow-season-in-canada

Miyo Pimatisiwin Productions. "Pow Wow Xperience." Video, 10:12. Storyhive, 2018. youtube.com/watch?v=Kgm1HKPFzlc

## Chapter Three

*Print*:

Pheasant, Karen. *The Promise to the Nokomis: The Transfer of the Anishinaabe Kwe Dance to the Next Generation.* Author, 2010.

Rendon, Marcie. *Powwow Summer: A Family Celebrates the Circle of Life.* St. Paul, MN: Minnesota Historical Society Press, 2013.

Smith, Cynthia Leitich. *Jingle Dancer.* New York, NY: Morrow Junior Books, 2000.

*Online*:

Pheasant, Karen. "It's All in the Song." *Windspeaker*, 2006. ammsa.com/publications/windspeaker/its-all-song

Ryan, Finn. "Powwow Trail: Keeping the Beat." Video, 4:40. *The Ways*, 2018. theways.org/story/powwow-trail

## Chapter Four

*Print*:

Marra, Ben. *Powwow: Images along the Red Road.* New York, NY: Harry N. Abrams, 1996.

Treuer, A. *Everything You Wanted to Know about Indians But Were Afraid to Ask.* St. Paul, MN: Borealis Books, 2012.

*Online*:

A Tribe Called Red. "Electric Pow Wow Drum." Video, 4:05. 2011. youtube.com/watch?v=lpkUISUx3Lo

"Life on the Rez: Powwow Performance." Video, 3:52. *Our America with Lisa Ling*, 2012. youtube.com/watch?v=CIree5hYe7A

# INDEX

*Page numbers in* **bold** *indicate an image; there may also be text related to the same topic on that page*

# Acknowledgments

First, miigwech to my parents for taking me out as a child to dance when powwows were not popular and were so far and few between. Thank you and hiy hiy to those old-school emcees who speak of the old stories about why we gather to uphold our old ways.

Miigwech/Ĩsniyė to the singers and dancers who maintain the integrity of our ways, and to all my dancing and singing friends with whom I have sat over the years, sharing stories that keep us strong as a people. Thank you to Jeannette Armstrong, who believed in me as a writer long before I did, and to Richard Van Camp for supporting and encouraging me.

To Orca Book Publishers, thank you for seeing beyond the aesthetics of powwow culture to the value and importance of doing this book. And thank you Andrew Wooldridge, Sarah Harvey and, most important, Merrie-Ellen Wilcox for your patience and understanding and for bringing in the work of Greg Younging. I am filled with gratitude.

**Karen Pheasant-Neganigwane** is an Anishinaabe dancer, educator, writer, artist and orator from Wiikwemkoong on Manitoulin Island, Ontario. Her grandparents, maternal and paternal, come from Wiikwemkoong. Her parents are residential school survivors. Karen is a PhD candidate in Educational Policy Studies/Indigenous Peoples Education at the University of Alberta. She is an Assistant Professor at Mount Royal University in the Treaty Seven region and is cross appointed to the Department of General Education, Office of Teaching and Learning, and the Department of Humanities–Indigenous Studies. Karen lives in Calgary.

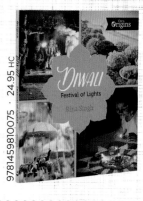
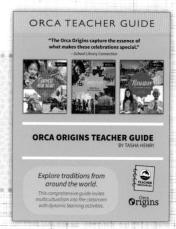